*I dedicate this book to the memories of
Danny Rosenheck, father of my youth,
and his cousin, David, father of my adulthood.*

*They were creative, melancholic, funny,
joyful and deeply good men.*

The Five Books of Limericks

A chapter-by-chapter retelling of the Torah

Rhonda Rosenheck

Teaneck, New Jersey

THE FIVE BOOKS OF LIMERICKS ©2022 Rhonda Rosenheck. All rights reserved. No part of this book may be used or reproduced in any manner whatsoever without written permission except in the case of brief quotations embodied in critical articles and reviews.

Published by Ben Yehuda Press
122 Ayers Court #1B
Teaneck, NJ 07666

http://www.BenYehudaPress.com

To subscribe to our monthly book club and support independent Jewish publishing, visit https://www.patreon.com/BenYehudaPress

Jewish Poetry Project #21　　　　　　　　　　http://jpoetry.us

Ben Yehuda Press books may be purchased at a discount by synagogues, book clubs, and other institutions buying in bulk. For information, please email markets@BenYehudaPress.com

ISBN13 978-1-953829-16-0

22 23 24 / 10 9 8 7 6 5 4 3 2 1　　　　　　　　　　20220929

Contents

Introduction	ix
Notes	xv
Acknowledgements	xviii

Genesis

Bereisheet/In the beginning	2
No'ach/Noah	3
Lech-Lecha/Get going, you!	4
Vayeira/And he appeared	6
Chayei Sarah/Sarah's life	7
Toledot/Generations	8
Vayetze/And he went out	9
Vayishlach/And he sent	10
Vayeshev/And he settled	11
Miketz/At the end	12
Vayigash/And he drew near	13
Vayechi/And he lived	14

Exodus

Shemot/Names	18
Va'eira/And I appeared	19
Bo/Come	20
Beshalach/When he sent out	21
(The Ten Commandments, version one)	22
Mishpatim/Laws	23
Terumah/Offering	24
Ki Tisa/When you elevate	26
Vayachel/And he assembled	27
Pekudei/Accountings	28

Leviticus

Vayikra/And he called	32
Tzav/Command	33
Shemini/Eighth	34
Tazria/She bears seed	35
Metzora/Infected person	35
Acharei Mot/After the death	36
Kedoshim/Holy ones	36
Emor/Say	37
Behar/On the mount	38
Bechukotai/In My laws	38

Numbers

Bamidbar/In the wilderness	42
Naso/Elevate	42
Beha'alotecha/When you lift	43
Sh'lach Lecha/You, yourself, send	44
Korach/Korach	45
Chukat/Law of…	46
Balak/Balak	47
Pinchas/Phineas	47
Matot/Tribes	49
Masei/Journeys of …	49

Deuteronomy

Devarim/Words	54
Va'etchanan/And I pleaded	54
(The Ten Commandments, version two)	55
Eikev/As a result	55
Re'eh/See	56
Shoftim/Judges	57
Ki Teitzei/When you go out	59
Nitzavim/Standing (Witnessing)	61
Vayelech/And he went	61
Ha'azinu/Listen up	61
V'zot Ha'brachah/And this is the blessing	62
About the Author	64

Turn it and turn it,
for everything is in it.
Reflect on it and grow old
and gray with it.

—Ben Bag-Bag

God's plan made a hopeful beginning.
But man spoiled his chances by sinning.
We trust that the story
Will end in God's glory,
But at present the other side's winning.

—Oliver Wendell Holmes, Sr.

These books, for Abrahamic faiths,
Reveal in humankind God's face.
Our ancestors' flaws
Gave God grievous pause –
Put guidelines for living in place.

Introduction

Why the Five Books of Moses? Why limericks? Is this book heretical?

Excellent questions.

Why the Five Books of Moses?

I have reread the first five books of the Hebrew Bible – also called *Torah* (teaching), *Mikrah* (reading) and *Chumash* (five) – at least once a year all my adult life. You would think that by now I'd know every character, motif, song, conflict, admonition and command by heart. Yet each time I read the Five Books of Moses, something hits me as if for the first time.

The Five Books dictate rules on top of laws on top of "shalts" and "shalt nots" with little explanation. Basically, we have to make do with two reasons constantly repeated: ... *because you were slaves in the land of Egypt*; and ... *so that you and your children may prosper in the land that God promised Abraham*. History is told, promises are made with caveats and conditions – all for a purpose.

Ah, but what is that purpose?

The narrative is convoluted, rough. Nature is lawless. Protagonists (never mind villains) often show themselves to be dishonest, dismissive, cowardly, impulsive, sycophantic, self-righteous jerks, clearly in need of Divine guidance yet rarely willing to accept it. Fiery swords twirl around on their own. Fallen angels mate with humans. Frogs take over a kingdom. The earth swallows a pack of rebels. A guy wins God's covenant of peace by skewering a couple *in flagrante delicto*. A smart ass talks back. Moses dies spitting distance from his goal. The Lord flies into rages at His* beloved Hebrews, who swing between terror and resentment of their invisible God, with few sincere moments of gratitude.

The over-arching logic and meaning are not explicit. Each reader must deduce or infer those messages from textual details and omissions. Yet – this is the eternally complicating *yet* – each person is a unique decoding organism; only by chance against massive odds would two or more readers understand identical messages. So, what is the goal?

Reading the Five Books differs completely from, say, reading a novel. We read the narrative every year; there should be no suspense. When I was a student at the Jewish Theological Seminary (a quarter century ago), many people knew that I loved to read mysteries. One morning, a classmate sat beside me as I was paging through a *chumash*, leaned over and whispered, "He dies in the end." My friend** was pretending to spoil suspense that neither of us would experience, because the purpose of reading Torah is not to see what happens next. The last poem I wrote for Deuteronomy opens with this long-germinating seed: "He died in the end, the great Moses." One mystery of the Five Books is that chronology is mutable. In imitation of my source material, what presents itself as the end of this book was, in truth, its beginning.

Is the point of reading to empathize with the characters? Probably yes, in part. But to what end? Maybe we should be jotting down all 613 directives; after all, many of us do ask the Bible how we should live. It stretches reason to conclude that we – here and now – should precisely follow directions designed for early humans and ancient Hebrews.***

---

* Yes, "His." This depiction of God is as toxic-masculine as it gets: *I love you, now do exactly as I say or I'll wipe the floor with you.*

** If you were that witty and delightful person, please remind me so I can give credit where it's due.

*** Three tangential thoughts: 1. Karaites are a now-tiny sect that does strive to

The splendid truth is, no one knows for whom, by Whom (whom), how or why the Five Books of Moses were written. Every theory is flawed, or at least unproven. Me? I love that I always fail, to some measure, when striving to plumb these fathomless words. Those failures, combined with tiny victories of understanding, thrill me. I never grow tired of the not-knowing.

Why Limericks?

Here too, no proven origin theory has emerged, but this is what I've learned. Limericks might have come into use as early as the 1600s and began to appear broadly in the 19th century. London writer Edward Lear popularized the form without naming it in *A Book of Nonsense* (1846). The name almost certainly refers to Ireland's County Limerick (*Luimneach*) or its seat, but originally denoted a different form of ditty that fell away as these limericks came into common use. Limericks came to reflect the Irish people's famously wry worldview.

Limericks are folk art, perfect for drunken poetry face-offs. They transgress taboos. The best of them have content that is bawdy or scatological and shows the protagonist to be foolish. Prim ones, lacking even subtle double *entendres* or other mischief, have long been disdained by lofty writers, most notably George Bernard Shaw.

When I was twenty-three, an older cousin and I sat at her kitchen table drinking sherry. We began reciting impromptu limericks about each

---

follow Biblical instructions literally. 2. Translating Biblical instructions for each generation's contemporary concerns is a central purpose of about 2500 years of rabbinic literature (rejected by the Karaites, who branched off as a result). 3. Some Christian testament was crafted to simplify daily life by replacing Torah's legal encumbrances with faith.

other. Here's the one I remember "about" me:*

There once was a woman named Rhonda
Who wanted to screw in a Honda.
But she was too tall,
Her car was too small,
So of Cadillacs she became fonda.

The one I remember reciting was inferior, being mischievous but not bawdy:

There was a young woman named Bobby,
Who wished to engage in a hobby.
She knit robes for her cat,
For each chair in her flat,
And for all of the guards in the lobby.**

Limericks, like Yiddish curses, serve as coded expressions of disdain for life endured under a self-congratulatory ruling class. The Five Books ooze land grabs, nocturnal emissions, cowardice, incest, lying, stealing, gluttony, sneakiness, prostitution, coercion, betrayal, injustices, revenge, perversions, disgusting illnesses, pimping, kidnapping, adultery, murders, maiming, magical thinking and blatant disdain for leaders with inflated egos and too much power. In sum, they are a limerick writer's dream.

Though most contemporary poetry (including mine) exists outside the constraints of fixed structures, historical poetic forms inspire me as vessels inspire filling. Each one begs me for different content. When writing haiku, I seek the inhale of a thought and its exhaled "Aha!"

---
* This *fictitious* limerick was conceived and recited by Roberta Brody, PhD. I drove Hondas for years; more than that, I'll never say.
** Today this is a trend called knit-bombing!

Rhonda Rosenheck

Sonnets pull elemental emotions from me. Ballads have me drawing out the story as I might around a campfire. Limericks beg me to point out something unsettling and lighten its load.

Here's my Genesis, Chapter One in haiku:

Gods starts to create,
separate, articulate.
Adam-Eve: know, see!

Here it is as a limerick:

From chaos began the creation,
Each flora and fauna its station.
The water and sky,
The earth they wind by,
Last Adam, who had to be patient.

The haiku's observations are rooted in the natures of language, being and consciousness. The limerick skims like a stone across the narrative, cheekily alluding to Adam's (and dare I say, his Creator's) flaws.

With this writing project, I wanted to have fun. Responding to each chapter by writing a limerick inspired me to dig quickly and no deeper than the top layer of meaning. These limericks do not always exploit a character's weakness directly; sometimes you'll need to apply peripheral vision. Lastly, not every poem in this collection is funny. Each chapter beckoned me somewhere different, and I followed.

Is this book heretical?

People who read only literal meanings and proof of their group's ascendency narrative in the Five Books of Moses will almost certainly find this book heretical. Luckily, they are unlikely to purchase a book titled *The Five Books of Limericks*. The rest of us can imagine that there exist many ways to shed light on these sacred texts. (If you are among the first set, maybe stop here, return the book and get your money back.)

I ascribe to an ancient metaphor that we should "turn it and turn it," endlessly studying the Torah this way and that, because we can learn something from everything about it. Each oddity, conundrum and textual (even calligraphic) anomaly beckoned ancient rabbis and teases contemporary scholars into searching for previously underived meanings.

That's what I did here. The intent of each poem is to share an (not *the*) essence of a chapter. I investigated each one to see what a lilting, poetic lens would magnify. Humor, revealing of human imperfection, is arguably essential in contemplating it. The opposite of heretical, these poems are a product of my enduring curiosity about and reverence for the Torah. Limericks are rarely expressions of awe, so I understand the confusion.

What I meant when writing matters less than what you now glean from reading; I pass the creative baton to each reader. I hope that the experience stimulates your imagination, discomfits you (just a little), gives you some laughs and pulls from you more than one *Aha!* I would love to hear your reflections. If we are not otherwise socially connected, please write to me through www.rhondarosenheck.com.

With blessings,

Rhonda Rosenheck
January 2022

Notes

Hazak, hazak va-nit'hazek: Be strong, be strong and strengthen ourselves

Repeating an ancient ritual, Jewish worshippers stand and recite this phrase after the final line of each of the Five Books is chanted. What it says to me is that the more we study these mysterious yet accessible texts, the stronger each individual becomes and the stronger the community can become, if we collectively intend it.

I wrote one *Hazak, hazak* limerick to close out the first four books and a different one to follow Deuteronomy.

Uses of Hebrew, Yiddish and more

Mostly, I chose Hebrew names over their English versions. The most significant name that might sound unfamiliar is "Moshe," the Hebrew from which the English name Moses derives. (Some posit that Moshe stems from an Egyptian word meaning "pull," as in Pharaoh's daughter pulled him out of the Nile.)

Some words fitted my mood or the limerick form better in Hebrew.

On other occasions, I couldn't resist the Yiddish, Spanish, French or Italian choice, or the Celtic, English or American-urban expression. Fear not; I translate each into American Standard English the first time it appears.

Poetic Structure

Limericks are a fixed form, consisting of five lines in the rhyme scheme *aabba*. This means that lines 1, 2 and 5 rhyme with each other while lines 3 and 4 rhyme with each other. Rhythm provides the lilt. Three iambs* shape lines 1, 2 and 5; lines 3 and 4 have two iambs each. A varying number of additional unstressed syllables is generally accepted.

As a personal challenge, I kept these limericks to syllable-sets of 8-8-5-5-8 or 9-9-6-6-9.

Parashah (Portion) vs. Chapter

Public readings of the Five Books probably took hold during Israel's Babylonian captivity, between 600 and 500 BCE. Chapter divisions were set much later, between the 13th and 15th century CE. (I'm too poorly versed in the evidence of ancient near-eastern history to take sides about exact dates, or even the real or mythical existence of anything I mention. Consider yourself forewarned not to rely on my historical explanations.)

The *parashot* are 54 standardized portions, sometimes combined, which ensure that the entire Torah is chanted each Hebrew, adjusted-lunar-calendar year. For those wishing to follow along weekly, I've included the name of each *parashah* above its first full chapter, in transliteration and translation.

While Torah scrolls include spaces and markings between *parashot*, chapters are noted only in bound – and many digital – editions. I based this project on chapters because 1/187th of the total represents fewer details than 1/54th, which made five-line summary-poems significantly less impossible to write.

---

*An iamb begins with a light syllable and concludes with an emphasized syllable, akin to the downbeat in music. It is the most common form of poetic "foot," meaning pattern of emphasis. Iambic pentameter (five iambs per line) might be the poetic structure closest to ordinary, conversational speech.

Liberties

I took liberties. I shortened words and names to fit. The word "Generation" became "gen." If rhythm or rhyme demanded it, Moshe got shortened to Mosh, Hagar to Gar, Moab to Mo, etcetera.

Mostly, I wrote in past tense, but when a line sounded better to me in present tense, I didn't fight it.

I exploited perfect hindsight and access to distant future references in my omniscient-narrator voice. Sometimes I reported the action neutrally, other times I judged. All derision is mine; please don't hold the early-readers, expecially not the nuns or rabbis, accountable for my attitude.

With rare and noted exceptions, each chapter includes only those narrative elements, actors, dictates and/or warnings found within that chapter. Often, I summed up an exchange with invented dialogue. I made up the words, but never whose words they might have been.

Lastly, I decided to demarcate mortal speech with quotation marks and allow God's speech to hover ambiguously. To ease the strain on your eyes when reading Deuteronomy, which is largely spoken by Moses to the Israelites, I used quotation marks only when Moses or the omniscient narrator is quoting another person.

Acknowledgements

For this project, I reread the Five Books of Moses online in Hebrew and English easily, thanks to Sefaria.org, a non-profit site offering a robust catalog of Jewish texts on a user-friendly platform.

Ben Yehuda Press publishes what's challenging and inventive and nearly forgotten in Jewish literature. I feel giddy – if famous, I'd have to say "humbled" – that this is being published as a volume of the Jewish Poetry Project.

My nephews, Daniel and Alec Rosenheck, edited early drafts of this book. Trained, nuanced copyeditors, they provided valuable feedback. Daniel-the-social-worker sharpened my prose while Alec-the-songwriter probed the gaps between my poetic intent and word choices. They are as demanding as Olympic coaches, though always kind. Imagine how motivating it is to read along a margin: "Auntie, you can do better!" Ben Yehuda Press poetry editor Julia Knobloch worked with me to ready the manuscript for publication.

Rabbi Patricia Fenton of American Jewish University read these limericks as they were being hatched. I kept writing because she kept laughing. Water-color painter Katharine Kernan, a former nun, was a full draft's first audience. She urged me to seek publication. Without these two friends, *The Five Books of Limericks* would not have gotten off the couch I sat on for a year writing compulsively, as if I was eating M&Ms.

My thanks for additional early reading and feedback go to Rabbis Avraham Ettedgui, Jeremy Gordon, Hillel Norry and Jon Spira-Savett, to Sister Francine Dempsey, and to these non-clerical readers: Linda Addison, Dianne Buja, Michael Dimant, Alison Gross, Jordy Gross, Professor Walter Herzberg, Elizabeth Massie, Markham Pyle and David Weiss. (I apologize if I've left someone out – I'm bound to have.) Found-object artist David Rosenheck and fellow creatives in three communities – Pyramid Lake Women's Writing Retreat, Stowe Writers Retreat and Creative Columbia Arts Salon – listened to me recite these limericks with enough appreciation to suggest that even people of good taste might enjoy them.

All my projects and activities benefit from the unswerving nurturance and delight Max H. Jacobs offers me daily. I so love this man who loves me so magnificently.

My thanks go to all of the above and more for egging me on.

Rhonda Rosenheck

Genesis

Was the world made for man or God?
Flood, plague and fire give hint a nod.
The garden was dear
Before human fear.
Abe's whole fam? Gritty, faithful, flawed.

1.   *Bereisheet*/In the beginning

From chaos began the creation,
Each flora and fauna its station.
The water and sky,
The earth they wind by,
Last Adam, who had to be patient.

2.

How, God-knows, some processes start.
Dew-mist and sweet rain played their part.
Gahn Eiden's* lush grown,
Beasts named. Man's alone:
A helpmeet for Adam seemed smart.

3.

Paradise. A serpent got loose
And gave the first woman a goose.
"All knowing you'll be;
Just eat from this tree."
Eve's blamed when they're nabbed for the ruse.

4.

Of two brothers' gifts, one was druthered.
No matter how well they were mothered,
Cain did poor Abel in,
And was marked for his sin.
Then Adam and Eve had another.

---

* Garden of Eden.

5.

Male and female, in this tale, were one.
This old Adam had Seth as a son.
Begettings begotten,
Not one gen forgotten,
Until Noah, from Lemach, was wrung.

6.

Amok ran all the people on earth,
Doing mischief and evil from birth.
An ark N. constructed.
His fam'ly's instructed:
Bring a pair of each critter to berth.

7. *No'ach*/Noah

A menagerie they assembled –
Sounds, odors – a zoo it resembled.
And then those rain-clouds burst.
Although they had rehearsed,
Rhinos, dodos and fleas all trembled.

8.

So long did they float on the water,
Days, nights, weeks, months all lost their order.
With a thundering crash,
Into Ararat bashed!
Stumbled out birds, beasts, sons and daughters.

9.

'Spite rainbows and forever promise,
N's clan and he suffered from traumas.
Here was "best of his gen,"
Drunk right out of his ken,**
Descending to nudism dramas.

10.

Ham's offspring, like Canaan: accursed!
For nations and power they'd thirst.
From Japheth through Shem,
Lands stretched eastward beyond the Thames.**
They peopled the whole universe.

11.

Folks tried unified existence.
Built skyscraper, showed persistence.
God scrambled each tongue,
Far distances flung!
Abe started clay-god resistance.

12. *Lech-Lecha*/Get going, you!

Trekked: Haran; Canaan toward Egypt.
Pharaoh's interest in Sarah was swift.
"Be my sister," Abe pled.
"Your good deed; I'm not dead."
But plagues scuttled the scheme and they drift.

---

* Conscious knowing
** England's Thames River is not mentioned in the Five Books; this is all me, indicating "farther than the eye can see."

13.

Too cramped, Lot's and Abe's men squabble.
"Why not move east for less trouble?"
Lot moved down to S'dom.
Abe's eyes eastward roamed:
His is the horizon, double.

14.

City-state kings took to warrin',
Took Lot with S'dom and G'morreh.
Abe's troops saved the day,
G'mor's king said, "I'll pay."
Abe refused this deal abhorrent.

15.

Abe's promised seed beyond number.
First, four gens will be encumbered.
Then out they will run,
A nation become,
The land God willed them, reenter.

16.

Barren Sarai's* handmaid subbed in.
Seed planted, she acted like kin.
Sarai gave her hell!
She fled to a well,
But was told to march right back in.

---

* Sarai is Sarah's name before she and Abram took the "h" at the end of their names to indicate attachment to God.

17.

Abe's told: Of *kind'lach** there'll be no dearth.
"Sarah's womb!?" Abe is dizzy with mirth.
"At our ages?" he asked.
"Fertile days have not passed!?"
Abe's offspring shall inhabit the earth.

18.   *Vayeira*/And he appeared

Abe invited three strangers to feast,
Whose words Sarah believed not the least.
In a hectic plot turn,
Abe pleads, "S'dom cannot burn!"
Agreed: If there're ten good men, I'll cease.

19.

Lot opened his home to two strangers,
Who told him to run from new dangers.
His wife turned back with rue
(She could season your stew).
His girls bedded him for his rangers.**

---

* Yiddish for children
** Perhaps thinking they were the only humans left to seed a new generation. Though, the daughters were raised in an immoral society. They were just pimped out by their dad within our hearing! Do we firmly believe that they initiated incest with Lot, who's known to be selfish and slick? I say it's more than fair to wonder whether this episode was written through ye-olde, "Justify-the-male-authority-figure-at-all-costs" lens.

20.

(At it again!) "Sar's my sister."
Abimelech wouldn't kiss her.
"Stop doing this, Abe,"
Abi said, then gave
Shekels to Abe, who had missed her.

21.

Isaac was born and snipped and weaned;
Half bro Ish and 'Gar* fled the scene.
As promised, they're saved–
Great future paths paved.
Abe, Abi cool their army's spleen.

22.

"*Hineini*" (Here!) called this father,
To God, Isaac, then another.
A sacrifice placed ...
A ram in Ike's place!
All while an angel did hover.

23.   *Chayei Sarah*/Sarah's life

Sarah died of old age (or of grief).
A loss from which Abe felt no relief.
With Hittites he haggles:
That cave for some shekels.
Machpelah's the field Sarah's beneath.

---

* Ishmael – Abraham's eldest son – and his mother, Hagar.

24.

"For my Isaac find a good fit,"
'S how Abe's servant understood it.
Met Isaac's cousin,
"Wow, she's so lovin'."
Rebecca swooned; Ike was worth it.

25.

Becca's womb, two nations struggling.
Hunter. Gentle. Twins she's juggling.
"Give your soup; I thirst!"
"Cede your birthright first!"
Thus, the fam'ly began crumbling.

26.   *Toledot*/Generations

Famine! So they joined Philistines,
Ike called "Sister" to avoid scenes.
Old Abi yelled, "No!?"
"*Et tu**, lying so?"
To Beer-Sheva they stole off, clean.

27.

Bro, mom were annoyed by E's wives.
With blessings at stake, they're at knives.
Jake cheated with stew.
Esau: "Bless *me*, too!"
Becca sent Jake far, for their lives.

---

* "You, too?" as in the last words Shakespeare pulls from Julius Caesar as his friend Brutus stabs him to death: *et tu, Brute?*

28.

Ike: "Marry a cousin like I did."
Esau wed Ishmael's grandkid.
Jake lammed to Padan
To meet girls of Laban.
Angel-ladder dream, Jake's mind blasted!

29.   *Vayetze*/And he went out

For Rachel, Jake fell head o'er heels.
At seven years, Labe heard appeals.
The wedding's a trick,
Leah's *taken the mick*...*!
For Rach, Jake must reap se'en more yields.

30.

Tricksters alike, Jake met his match,
Though he won a great haul to catch:
Two wives 'stead of one,
One girl, 'leven sons!
Plus, healthiest sheep of the batch.

31.

His clan tiptoed off unannounced,
Rightly feared Laban's urge to pounce.
They met at Beth-El,
Their anger to quell.
Rach's skirts (hiding gods) did not flounce.

---
* Tricked

Five Books of Limericks   9

32.

Jake sent word and gifts to Esau,
Prayed in fear, admitting his flaw.
With angel he strove,
Bruised thigh, though he dove.
Limped off in the morning, more sure.

33. *Vayishlach*/And he sent

Jake and Esau approached ... and embraced!
Each one's over-polite to his face.
Hold anger, what's the use?
At least now there's a truce.
Israel and clan moved to a new place.

34.

Sister Dinah is "*known*" by Shechem,
Odious news! Her bros plan mayhem:
"Sh'chem!* Get snipped to hook up."
Lust-blind, "Agreed!" Set up:
Post mass-bris, the brothers attacked them.

35.

Israel's clans called back to Beth-El:
Renew your faith! It never gelled.
Ben's born on the way,
Rach died the same day.
Old Isaac? To ancestors fell.

---

* Shechem names the leader, his people, and their place.

36.

A nation emerged from Esau,
More nations from that, as we saw.
Off from Jake he roamed.
He fathered Edom,
Chieftains from Se'ir to Bozrah.

37.   *Vayeshev*/And he settled

Young Joseph was spoilt, so it seemed.
Self-'grandizing omens he dreamed.
Bros resented it;
They carved him a pit
(And dug *themselves* one with this scheme).

38.

Judah married a Canaaness.
Their sons had bad luck – more than less.
Lev'rite-pledged T'mar,*
Big M** in her stars,
Tricked pop-in-law, Judah, to beds.

---

* When Judah's son died before Tamar had children, she was pledged to the next brother down. When he died childless, she was pledged to the next one down, who was too young a lad.
** Menopause! And, yes, "tricked." Tamar disguised herself as a prostitute; Judah picked her up along the road for some cheap nooky.

Five Books of Limericks

39

Joe, the valet extraordinaire,
Trusty hunk, dodged Ms. Potifaire.
She grabbed him. He fled.
"He raped me," she said.
Jailed, then boss of everyone there.

40

Royal baker, butler were sacked,
Put in jail. King thought, "Who'll be back?"
Their dreams Joseph read:
Who'll live, who'll be dead.
(Though right, no one heard of his knack.)

41. *Miketz*/At the end

Two years on, Pharaoh dreamt two dreams,
Asked around, what each of them means.
"Joseph will know it."
Joe: "Plan not to blow it:
"Seven fat years, then seven leans."

42.

Ten brothers begged Big Man on Nile.
They'd all eaten naught in a while.
Joe wept. Slyly preyed:
"Bring youngest!" Shim* stayed.
Jake: "No! Ben goes nowhere hostile!"

---

* Shimon (Simon)

43.

When food stores ran dry, Jacob said,
"Fetch more corn," forgetting the threat.
Bros went back with gifts,
Young Ben in their midst.
(Gets a pass, their aid-and-abet?)

44.

(Not yet!) "Hide my cup in Benjie's sack.
"Aide, go find that loot and bring them back!"
Indignation exceeds;
Judah begs, Judah pleads.
"Take *me* in trade, lest old Jake be wracked."

45.   *Vayigash*/And he drew near

"I'm him whom you tossed," said Joe. "Forsooth,
"It was Divine strategy, in truth.
"Bring our father to me,
"Take the best you can see,
"Gone, hunger and scrabbling nail and tooth."

46.

Clan father Jake rode to green Goshen,
Led flocks, sixty-six kin in motion.
Cried, "Joseph, my son!
"Has this good day come?"
Like swigging some wake-from-haze potion.

47.

Jacob and king, like old friends, schmoozed.*
Joe traded land, bread; none refused.
"Sell all to the king!
"A fifth each must bring,
"Of all he planted, reaped and accrued."

48.   *Vayechi*/And he lived

On deathbed, Jake blessed Joseph's heirs,
Menash, 'Phrayim** get tribal shares.
"The best is blessed first,
"Not order of birth.
"Both will grow, be brave and well fare."

49.

With harsh truths, Jake "blessed" his flawed sons,
Ass! Snake! Judah'll rule all you bums.
"Take me to that cave,
"Where my kin are saved,"
Said Jacob 'fore his breath's last runs.

50.

Nile custom upheld: embalmed Jake first.
Ride to Efron in paleo-hearse.
Bereft brothers feared Joe,
Whose kindness grew more so.
Joe died; his corpse embalmed and traversed.

---

* hung out and chatted, in Yiddish.
** Menashe and Ephraim (Splitting Joseph's share, they become numbers 11 and 12 of the Tribes of Israel.)

Hazak, Hazak va-Nit'hazek

Be strong, be strong and strengthen ourselves.

We're strengthened by studying Torah.
This book taught us more than we thoughta.
So stand and be strong,
Do right more than wrong,
And start the next book that's before ya.

Exodus

A leader arose who knew not …;
Caught Hebrews in a narrow spot.
In kiln hot as hell
Israel gained a shell,
Roamed 'til ex-enslaved ones begot.

1. *Shemot*/Names

Goshen filled up with folks Hebrew.
Flocks that teemed and fam'lies that grew.
A new king arose:
"Save sisters, kill bros!"
But God-awed midwives saved boys too.

2.

Ark launched – of pitch, slime and cattail.
Babe's sis set it a'Nile to sail,
Drawn out by a queen,
Royal lad! 'Til he's seen:
"*Murderer!*" To Midian he'd bail.

3.

Moshe met I'll-Be-what-I'll-Be
At an unconsumed, fiery tree.
Go stop their despair,
Hebrew slaves down there.
Lead'm out to milk and honey.*

4.

Mosh can't make an obstacle stick:
Price on his head? Tongue that's not slick?
Aaron will join you,
King'll ignore you,
'Spite your pleas and cool magic tricks.

---

* This is not where the land is said to flow with milk and honey. I stole it for the rhyme.

5.

"Let Israel go, pray for three days."
Pharaoh refused. "Your people stays!"
Bitter from labor,
"*Feh!* You're no savior!"
Mosh to God, "Plan's going sideways."

6.

Mosh worked to persuade the enslaved,
Who sneered at him, "*Sure* we'll be saved!"
Noting roll call
Of kinsmen and all,
Mosh begged off, but God was unfazed.

7. *Va'eira*/And I appeared

Mosh'n Aaron went to the king:
Epic show of Divine meddling.
Turned Nile into blood
With tap of a rod,
Plagued Egypt; frogs galore hopping.

8.

Pharaoh's heart's too hard to let go,
More plagues promised; Pharaoh was slow.
Lice made them all itch,
And flies made them twitch.
But each 'tempt to leave was struck low.

9.

"At dawn, your cows will die. Not mine;
"Israel's livestock will fare just fine.
"Next, furnace ash
"Will raise boils worse than rash."
Pharaoh still won't budge from his line.

10.   *Bo*/Come

I've hardened that egotist's heart.
To generations you'll impart
That *I* got them out,
Not that Pharaoh lout,
Not even you, doing your part.

11.

Rebellion set in, king's ire grows,
Ambivalence, shouting "Git!"s and "No!"s.
Hail pounded their fields,
Locusts consumed yields.
In darkness king says: "*Adiós!*"*

12.

Word came down: "Now Israel, listen!
"Feast on lamb while dressed to hasten."
First-born 'gyptians died.
King wailed, cried "Go! Fly!"
Israel ran, enriched (though chastened).

---

* They did not speak Spanish in Ancient Egypt. What wouldn't I do for a rhyme?

13.   *Beshalach*/When he sent out

"Children! Consecrate. Meditate
"That your Lord did not hesitate.
"God brought us all out
"With great Divine clout.
"Never forget your enslaved state."

14.

Israel needs much more trust in Me.
Pharaoh's wrath again I'll set free.
God split the water,
King's army? Slaughtered!
Folks could not believe what they see.

15.

Wild song 'n dance: "Our en'my's crushed!
With Lord's right hand, to depths they're thrust!"
(Israel's joy, my dear,
Was short-lived, I fear.)
Water bitter? To *kvetch** they rushed.

16.

Two point five months in, camped at Sin.
Starved, Israel wailed, "You did us in!"
Mosh: "I'm at a loss.
"Complain to the Boss."
God let the gift of mahn** begin.

---
* Yiddish, to complain vociferously. Literally, it means "squeeze." Don't you love that?
** Manna, the mysterious nutritional substance that God provided daily.

17.

'Long Refidim trek, protest staged.
"You're kvetching again?" Moshe raged,
Then smacked a dry spring
(An unsanctioned thing).
Amalek attacked young and aged.

18.   *Yitro*/Jethro

Jethro with M's fam'ly appeared,
And praised God, after all he heard.
Reunion so sweet!
In thought they retreat,
To plan a court system revered.

19.

"God brought you here on eagles' wing."
Folks fenced away from mountain's ring.
"Wash up and hands off,
"While I hike aloft."
God: Don't let them touch anything!

20.   (The Ten Commandments, version one*)

I brought you out. Idols? For shame!
I'm jealous. Don't squander My name.
Rest one day a week,
Give parents no cheek,
Don't murder, cheat, yearn, or defame.

---

* *You* try conveying the Ten Commandments in 34 syllables! Really, try it. Send it to me through rhondarosenheck.com.

21.   *Mishpatim*/Laws

Bought a servant? So set them free.
Kill? Be killed. When it's *oops*, then flee.
Don't hurt each other,
Though foe or lover;
You'll pay a price equal, you'll see!

22.

Holy? Don't cheat, conjure or steal,
Something happen? Tell it for real.
Rape? You'll pay the price.
To weakest be nice.
Give Me thanks. (And carrion's no meal.)

23.

Steer clear of lies and wicked crowd
Help all who fall or cry aloud.
Come see Me thrice-year.
Kid? In milk don't sear.
Heed my angel, leading you proud.

24.

Hebrews listen then nod. "We're down."*
Mosh splattered blood, so they were bound.
Leaders climbed halfway.
On sapphires they'd wait
For Mosh to descend from the cloud.

---

* We're down, meaning we're up … for this – ready, willing and able. English can be so much fun!

25. Terumah/Offering

Mosh saw the blueprint, the décor,
Gold-winged k'ruvim* down to the floor.**
People's heart-felt gifts
The holiness lifts.
To God's place, folks came to adore.

26.

'Broidered linen curtains to spec,
In loops and swirls and sweeping breadth.
Metal fittings bold,
Brass, silver and gold.
Acacia beams, tenoned for strength.

27.

Craft the altar with precise care,
And the courtyard all around there.
Pillared and gated,
Wood (metal-plated).
Brass offering-tools, oil a'flare.

---

* Cherubim, but not the sweet baby-angels of ceramic *tchotchkes*** and Valentine's Day cards. These were tall, gaunt, gold-winged, non-humanoid, solemn angels that protected the ark, like God's own Swiss Guard.
** *Tchotchkes*: Yiddish for decorative doo-dads that collect dust.

28. *Tetzaveh*/You shall command

Aaron and sons will be the priests.
Donning ephod, robe, tunic (pieced),
Linen-cotton twists –
Just this once, *shatnez*!*
Twelve-gem breastplate: Tribes' vibes released.

29.

Consecrate your nephews and bro,
Priesthood etern', do it just so:
Bring matzahs and meats
To grill Me a feast.
Anoint their heads with oil a'flow.

30.

Incense-altar Israel erects,
Sweet aromas the fire projects.
To atone feels so nice.
(Just don't bring strange spice!)
Crowd-fund it with half-shekel tax.

---

* *Shatnez* is the blending of linen (plant-product) and wool (animal-product) for clothes. In my view, it's one of the "Don't act too God-like" prohibitions, same as not co-opting the life-power of blood. *Shatnez* and blood use, representations of Divine power, are forbidden for everyday use, yet required in sacrificial rites. (That the Hebrew word for these rites, *korban*, literally means "draw near" strengthens my case.)

31.   *Ki Tisa*/When you elevate

I'm sending you the man with the plan,
Skilled to craft it all, tent-flaps to pan.
Betzalel is his name,
Spirit-gifted? Insane!
Keep Sabbath. Mosh gets tablets in hand.

32.

"Woe is us! That dude's gone for good!"
Calf-idol, stiff-necks understood.
God let Moshe know;
Aar'n shrugged, saying, "So?
"Most folks don't act good as they should." *

33.

Angry Lord gives Self a time-out,
Moshe pleads, "You're with me, no doubt?"
In a tent they meet,
So to be discreet.
Plan upcoming Face-to-back bout.

34.

Hew two stone tabs like those you smashed,
I'll keep my pledge, though Israel sassed.
If it's first, it's Mine,
Be it fig or kine.**
Don't fall for Ites' false god or lass.***

* At which point, Moshe smashes the tablets in a fit of pique.
** cattle
*** *Ites* is my English shorthand for peoples, in this case local ones known for

35.   *Vayachel*/And he assembled

Israel: Get down to brass (gold) tacks,
It's past time to clean up your acts.
Work Sabbath? A sin!
Call artisans in
To build tent, from vision to facts.

36.

Betzalel/Oholiav lead
All craftsmanship, each loop and bead.
Donations? Enough
To build all the stuff,
And sew the plush curtains they need.

37.

Storage ark, acacia and gold
With cherubs carved, tablets to hold.
Tools and an altar,
No craftsmen faltered,
Down to oils, with spicing so bold.

38.

Obeyed Divine plan to craft them.
Tent-curtains, woven and fine hemmed.
Grand accoutrements
They formed, like savants,
From pure metals Israelites sent.

---

particularly egregious-to-God modes of worship and warring, e.g. Canaanites and Moabites.

Pekudei/Accountings

39.

Next, the priest's clothing they fashion:
Tunics, with bells and a sash on.
Breastplate, gem-crusted,
Gold crown entrusted.
Each item passed expectation.

40.

Moment had come. Beta-test use:
Erect. Offer. Drape tunics loose.
The tent that's for Me
Gets clouds of glory,
Which lift when you're meant to vamoose.

Hazak, Hazak va-Nit'hazek
Be strong, be strong and strengthen ourselves.

We're strengthened by studying Torah.
This book taught us more than we thoughta.
So stand and be strong,
Do right more than wrong,
And start the next book that's before ya.

Leviticus

Offering-modes to death-judgment,
Decode these to learn what I meant:
In re: man, earth, Me,
Do good, feel lucky.
I own this land to you I lent.

1.   *Vayikra*/And he called

From God's tent came these instructions,
Burning meat for holy unctions.
Pinch pigeons at neck;
Steer must be perfect.
Grilled, smoked – barbeque eruptions!

2.

With grains, this is a different deal,
Be they baked, fried or ground to meal.
Just one part is burned.
The rest, Aaron earned.
(Serve with fine herbs and olive oil.)

3.

Peace-gifts? Kidneys – fat (adipose*)
From your best lambs, cows and/or goats.
Put hand on its head
Before it is dead.
Let priests scatter blood on the posts.

4.

And when you've messed up by mistake
Sin-atonement offer I'll take.
Bulls for priests and all,
Goats for leaders tall.
Poor schnook?** Goat- *or* lamb-offer make.

  * Yes, this is that dangerous-on-humans, dense fat that packs in around the organs.
  ** A schnook is a fool or a sad-sack. The text calls him "a soul" in contrast to

Rhonda Rosenheck

5.

False witness, one touching *tamei*,*
Or evil oath-maker, let's say:
Give by spending pow'r,
Goat, two birds, fine flour ....
A bumbler, with shekels can pay.

6.   *Tzav*/Command

Stoke a hot wood fire through the night.
Bring ash to a clean place off-site.
Keep the flames going,
And embers glowing.
(Priests sure earn those food-shares, alright!)

7.

Guilt offering is most holy.
Smell of smoke makes stomachs growly.
No adipose fat,**
Forbidden – that's that!
For My gift, burn beasts up wholly.

---

a prince. That contrast suggests to me compassion on ordinary people, aka my poor schnooks, whose work enriches the princes. They rate some rare Divine flexibility.
* People or things in a ritually impure state (and the impure state itself). Generally, contamination is through contact with blood or a dead body.
** The same organ-packing fat that is *prescribed* above is *proscribed* here. No, I haven't formed a theory.

8.

Pilot offerings! They assemble
At God's tent flap, all a'tremble.
Aaron/sons got dressed
In priestly finest
For first rites at Tabernacle.

9. *Shemini*/Eighth

Day eight, they sacrificed anew,
Priest's sin: bull. Then calf, ox, lamb, ewe.
Blood of each, horn-dashed.
Bones, hide: burned to ash.
Holy, crackling flames their minds blew!

10.

A's sons paid poor heed, gifted wrong.
Fire devoured them; message sent strong.
Leave tears to the crew.
Invest the next two.
No booze when representing throng.

11.

Divide 'tween impure and "That's fine."
Animals? Eat permitted kind:
Split hooves and chew cud
(No frogs or pigs' blood),
Scaled-finned fish, insects that hop high.

12. *Tazria*/She bears seed

New mom's impure one week, one mon',
Surgery on day eight for her son.
For girls, longer stay:
Two weeks, 66 days.
Offer gifts when natal blood's gone.

13.

Leprosy is an impure state,
As boil or on skin and bald pate.
States of symptoms count:
Stay in? Get sent out?
(Grows on cloth too, warp, woof and plait.)

14. *Metzora*/Infected person

Return to camp, 'neath your lintel,
Wash and shave; inspect each pimple.
Wait outside tent door,
'Til you're cleared as pure.
Leprosy treatment? Not simple.

15.

What to do with human issue?
Genital flow, leaked *in situ*.
Impure! *Blech!* Unclean!
Where it's now or been?
Love? Stay apart, though they miss you.

16.   *Acharei Mot*/After the death

Two sons dead, at God's tent Aar'n atones
For self, tent and Israel, with two goats.
Kill one – razzle-dazzle!
Shove one off – Azazel!
Israel clears its sin-slate through the Koh'ns.*

17.

Now hear this, sacrificers all:
Meeting-tent door or nowhere 'tall.
No more wantonness
With gods, goddesses.
Eat no flesh if beast's hunted, falls.

18.

Don't follow Egypt or Canaan.
Follow *My* laws, each to a man.
'Void taboos, per list,
Don't lie with man, beast.
I'll puke willful 'Ites from the land.

19.   *Kedoshim*/Holy ones

Be holy as am I, Israel,
Honor parents, keep Sabbaths well.
Save food for the poor,
Don't be rapist, boor,
Tattooed, thief, pimp, charmer with spells.

---

* Kohens, priests

20.

Give Molech* seed? You're dead to Me!
Live or not, you're shunned completely.
Forbidden couplings
Are the most troubling.
Abhorrence? Or milk 'n honey?

21.   *Emor*/Say

Priests abide by stricter constraint.
Purity, rotting corpses taint.
Don't shave or rend clothes,
No harlots – God knows!
Bachelors? Your tasks concentrate.

22.

A's sons eat well – once cleaned that is,
Pure (after nighttime emishs).
They can't touch a bug,
Leper, carrion blood.
Bring high quality, Grade-A gifts.

23.

Israel: Keep your dates with the Lord,
Sabbath, Passover. *D'accord?***
Weeks. Then Ram's-Horn Day,
Atone. In booths stay.
When reaping, leave corners to the poor.

---

* Canaanite god associated with child sacrifice
** *Agreed?* Ancient Israelites did not speak French. I, too, do not speak French.

Five Books of Limericks

24.

Cold press oil for eternal lamp,
Shabbos bread for priests from whole camp.
Blaspheme Me and die,
Else, pay eye-for-eye.
My laws're for all, native and tramp.

25.   *Behar*/On the mount

In the land, there'll be more limits,
Each earth-Sabbath, dust inhibits.
Half cen**? Debts erased
At prorated base.
Slaves? Their choice. Awe, you'll exhibit.

26.   *Bechukotai*/In My laws

Israel, the future's in your hands,
Dwell at home or in en'my lands.
Abhor laws? You'll see,
You'll plead for mercy.
I'm here, once you heed My commands.

27.

When you volunteer gifts, beware:
Once uttered, obligation's clear.
Take-backs will cost you
A shekel or two.
Some vows keep you ever ensnared.

---

*   cen(tury)

Hazak, Hazak va-Nit'hazek

Be strong, be strong and strengthen ourselves

We're strengthened by studying Torah.
This book taught us more than we thoughta.
So stand and be strong,
Do right more than wrong,
And start the next book that's before ya.

Numbers

For now, you're in the wilderness.
You're trying hard but make a mess.
Count up, be ready,
Formation steady.
I'll make it clear when you transgress.

1.   *Bamidbar*/In the wilderness

Start counting the men who can fight,
From twenty and up – get it right!
Six hundred, three thou,
But Levites leave out.
'Round meeting tent they're to hang tight.

2.

East is Judah's, Zeb's and Issech's.
Shimon, Gad, Reuben? South, not west,
Where Menasheh, Ben
And 'Phryam you'll send.
For Asher, Napht' and Dan, north's best.*

3.

'Member Aaron's first sons, found dead?
Next two sons became priesthood's head.
Levs: tend Kohens close
(Clean, sing, dress them, host),
In Israel's first-born sons' good stead.

4.

Eight thousand five hundred, four score
Levites tend the tent, peak to floor.
Each sub-clan its task,
Pillar, fabric, flask.
Males thirty to fifty: Report!

---

*Even I'm impressed, fitting all twelve tribes and four directions into 34 syllables!

5. *Naso*/Elevate

Be clear about keeping camp pure.
You're defiled or gross? Out the door!
Wife may have cheated?
Bad water'll be meted
If, jealously, husband adjures.

6.

Yearning for rites o'er and above?
Nazir* vows should fit like a glove.
No haircuts or grapes,
Or fun'rals to make.
Aaron? Bless folks: grace, peace and love.

7.

Twelve days, tribal princes brought gifts
Of such heft, took wagons to lift.
Who's it to impress,
This, at God's behest?
Moshe heard God's voice, got the gist.

8. *Beha'alotecha*/When you lift

Scrub these Levites clean with soap-cake.
Lieu first-borns, by right I could take.
I'm fine with the trade
Israel and I made.
Levs serve like valets for priests' sake.

---

* Nazarite

9.

"Tainted from a corpse, what to do?"
Asked two men 'fore *Pesach** ensued.
Mosh checked with *Yud-Hey*.**
"Next month, then. Same day."
Break camp just as cloud lifts in view.

10.

Craft horns of silver, clear and loud,
Trumpet alarms, advance (with cloud).
Take care that each blast
Evokes action fast,
So your camp moves agile and proud.

11.

And then, flash! Discontent let loose.
God's ire blazed; Hebrews obtuse!
Mosh begged, "Just kill me!
"*I'm* not their Lord, see?"
God sent fowl 'til it cooked their goose.

12.

Mosh's sibs got in on the act,
"Who made *him* prince, in point of fact?"
This humble Mosh, here?
Is whom *I* draw near!
Journey stalled; Mir's leprosy-wracked.

---

* Passover
** *Yud-Hey* are the first two Hebrew letters of God's reportedly most holy name.

13.   Sh'lach Lecha/You, yourself, send

God said, "Send spies out – recon."
One per tribe scouted Cana'an:
Said, "They're huge in there,
"Don't know how we'd dare!"
'Cept Caleb and Joshua ben Nun.

14.

Their weeping-crazed rebellion got real.
"Keep the faith!" No avail, this appeal.
The Lord flew into fits,
Mosh, your people's the pits!
(M makes God a Machiavellian deal.)

15.

When at last you enter My land …
(God listed the gifts He'd command).
You goof? Remedy.
Dis* God? Memory!
Stone that Sabbath-breaker by hand.

16.   Korach/Korach

Korach, two-fifty Levites brash.
"God dwells in us *all*!" (That so rash?)
Mosh planned a spice-off,
Warned folks to move off.
Earth sucked that coup down in a flash.

―――――――――
* Provocatively disrespect

Five Books of Limericks   45

17.

Grumblings became roars. Once more,
God resolved to destroy each boor.
Plague hit – quick encased –
Fourteen-thou erased!
Aaron's sons are priests evermore.

18.

Aaron, your sons, nephews are mine,
To serve holy roles for all time.
Diff'rentiate their tasks;
Levs, stay clear of flasks.
Fear not, you'll be cared for just fine.

19. *Chukat*/Law of...

Perfect red heifer, burn to ash.
With care, out of camp bring the stash
To re-purify
Those who touched who died.
Tamei: impure from a life passed.

20.

Miriam died at Midbar Tzin's mouth.
Aaron too (Mount Hor to the south).
Despite these losses,
Edom brought forces,
Blocking access through their king's route.

21.

More Israel/desert-clan conflict;
They can't lam so lickety-split.
Brass antidote-snake
Heals "no thanks" mistake.
Book of the Lord's Wars* tells it strict.

22.   *Balak*/Balak

Balak declares Hebrews the worst,
Sends Priest Balaam to have them cursed.
Said God: Don't go. OR go,
But speak by *My* say-so.
Smart ass – real one – sat un-coerced.

23.

Bullocks, rams on seven altars.
Balaam, paid to curse Israel, falters.
"God's blesseds, I bless,
"Jacob is God's best!"
"Look twice," king begged. "Your judgment, alter."

24.

Balaam: "How good are Israel's tents,
Jacob's dwellings, in this instance."
He read their future:
Victories, not torture,
'Gainst wanton nations, sent back whence ....

---

* Apparently there's a military chronicle of the Israelites' adventures that's been lost to humanity (until someone uncovers a remnant of it).

25.   *Pinchas*/Phineas

Israel turned to strange gods once more,
Bedded Moab for *Ba'al-Pe'or*.*
Mixed pair went to screw;
Pinchas stabbed them through!
(He won God's peace-pledge from that gore.)

26.

From the plague their philand'ring brought,
Census count was off by deaths caught.
Re-count families,
Each branch from all their trees.
Males plus Serach, who's Asher's daught' … er.

27.

Zelophehad's girls won the right:
Inherit (no male kin in sight).
Mosh, go climb a hill
And follow My will.
Josh will lead from here with his might.

28.

God craves barbeque aromas!
Gift-eat yourselves into comas:
Flour, wine, bullocks, lambs,
Each, its time and plans:
Shabbos, weekdays, guilty traumas.

---

* A Moabite god.

29.

Blow horns, afflict your souls; atone
By offering beasts' flesh and bone.
Fest'vals the reason,
Gifts for each season –
'Bove day's homage to the Throne.

30. *Matot*/Tribes

Gals, if dad/husband hears you vow,
He can annul it, or allow,
But must nullify
'Fore a day goes by.
Widows: swear any way and how.

31.

Revenge me on Midian, said the Lord.
Twelve thousand slayed and five kings; flames roared.
Saved only virgin girls,
Metal melts in fire, swirls.
Divvied loot, maidens, soldiers: God's hoard.

32.

Cattlemen-sons of Rueb' and Gad,
Craved pastures in Jazer-Gilyad.
"Let us settle here,
"Women, children, steer.
"We'll fight 'side you, as good comrade."

33.   *Masei*/Journeys of …

Their long Sinai trek's recorded,
From Egypt with "gifts" well-lauded.
Forty-one camp stops!
At Hor, Aaron drops.
From Mo*: Look! Homeland afforded!

34.

Moshe and God reconnoiter,
Mapping out each tribal border.
Divide up the land
Send each tribe's war-band
To conquer, each one, its quarter.

35.

Divvy by clan numbers fairly,
Give Levites cities and land free:
Six sanctuary,
Forty-two vary.
Blood defiled this land: so heed Me!

36.

"When girls who get land pass away,
Does inheritance shift or stay?"
"Good question," Mosh said.
"It stays once they're dead.
"From their dad's tribe they wouldn't stray."

---

* Moab, which abuts Canaan.

Hazak, Hazak va-Nit'hazek

Be strong, be strong and strengthen ourselves

We're strengthened by studying Torah.
This book taught us more than we thoughta.
So stand and be strong,
Do right more than wrong,
And start the next book that's before ya.

Deuteronomy

Tired Moshe offered this recap.
"Israelites, my energy's sapped.
"You're brutal to lead
"'S there no one you'll heed!?"
Then Mosh died. His era's a wrap.

1.   *Devarim*/Words

Leader Moshe retells the tale
Of when they'd listen, when they'd wail.
O'er forty years in,
Again they begin
(Ment'lly) down that Promised-Land trail.

2.

Of our travails, I'll remind you.
Adversaries strong, allies few.
We raided Sihon,
But skirted Ammon.
As God told us to – and not to.

3.

All cities of Bashan's King Og,
We conquered in our travelogue.
Hill country this side,
Assigned to Joe's pride,
Reub's and Gad's. Hear this apologue:

4.   *Va'etchanan*/And I pleaded

Israel, God chose you for His law.
Know it 'til it sweats from each pore.
Make your children see
How holy to be,
Or a wand'ring future's in store.

5. (The Ten Commandments, version two*)

I'm One! (Pledged to us alive now.)
Don't vain-talk. Don't worship a cow.
To parents be kind.
On Sabbath unwind.
Don't kill, steal, lie, covet, fool 'round.

6.

Take this land your en'mies prepared.
Do God's will with deep awe, a'feared.
Have no other gods.
Don't be nasty clods!
God freed you as slaves to thrive here.

7.

Know you'll win over nations great.
Israel, God's planning your'n their fate.
You're tiny, it's true –
God will protect you.
For loyalty, don't make God wait.

8.

God honed you with harsh desert sands
(Sustained with no work from your hands).
You're not who's so great,
God filled up your plate.
You'll perish, abhorred, from these lands.

---

* Another 34 syllable version. I dare you; bring yours on! Send it through rhondarosenheck.com.

9.   *Eikev*/As a result

You stiff-necked folk! Oft' I sent pleas
That God not cut you off at knees.
The promise He made,
To Jake, Isaac, Abe
Was: We'll replace resident sleaze.

10.

I had to carve stones three and four,
Dwell mountain-top forty days more!
God spared you His wrath.
Stop leaving the path!
Walk God's way: put others before.

11.

Tall and strong cross in. Possess it,
The land where God's rainfall wets it.
You saw the Lord's might.
Keep God's words in sight.
Teach your child, lest s/he forgets it.

12.   *Re'eh*/See

Smash their altars, their asherot.*
Give God the best of what He wrought.
Eat meat 'til you tip,
But blood? Not a sip.
They burned children! ('Gainst what God sought.)

---

* goddess statues

13.

Be clear: Their gods are forbidden.
Straying from yours won't be hidden.
Let none persuade you;
Don't do as they do.
In fact, stone 'em dead, good riddance!

14.

Eat mammals that chew and re-chew,
With hooves that are cloven in two,
Clean birds, I insist –
They're all on this list.
Carrion is not kosher for you.

15.

Yes, lend your money when they need,
With a heart that you've cleared of greed.
Seventh year, forgive!
God feeds and lets live.
Set Hebrew slaves free; God will heed.

16.

Come thrice a year, feast at God's place,
Sukkot, Weeks, when eating flat cakes.
Share your best and first,
Sate hunger, slake thirst.
(God's festivals run at mad pace!)

17.   *Shoftim*/Judges

Judge severe transgressions dearly,
Two witnesses' say so – fear Me.
With a dead-locked court,
Turn to priest cohort.
Anointed kings: Live austerely.

18.

Don't burn children, soothsay, divine:
Your worship methods shall be Mine.
New gen'ral you'll face
To take Moshe's place.
Forsake fakers for genuine.

19.

So innocent blood's not shed there,
Three cities you'll keep, havens where
Killers without hate
Live out a safe fate.
Bad actors? They'll pay all that's fair.

20.

Don't fear their armies; God's your sword!
Fiancé? Faint? "Stay home," says Lord.
Save fruit trees, a must.
Smash these folks to dust.
(War rules differ here from abroad.)

21.

Corpse en route; nearby city begs off!
Captive lovelies mourn shaved, in sack cloth.
Eldest's mom is hated?
'Herits twice what's fated.
Stone doomed son? As one, parents, come forth.

22.   *Ki Teitzei*/When you go out

Act to restore what kinsmen lose.
Don't hide in other gender's clothes.
Shoo bird-moms away.
Fence flat roofs today.
Lay with virgins? Pay! (No excuse.)

23.

Don't mess with your dad, stepmother.
Unlike Moab, Edom's your brother.
Night leak? Bury far.
Whores? Dogs? Temple barred.
Nosh – don't hoard – crops of another.

24.

Don't marry remarried ex-wife.
God brought you from bondage to life:
Don't exploit poor slaves
Or debtor you saved.
Obey this list; strive to be nice.

25.

Lash a crook forty, but not one more'n ....
Don't muzzle your oxen threshing corn.
Bros, wed SILs as Lev'rites,*
Wives can't grab balls in fights.**
Curse Amalek with eternal scorn.

26.   *Ki Tavo*/When you enter

Bring first fruits to God's tent with your tithe,
So the poor and God's servants don't writhe.
Tell our story again,
"Out of Egypt ... and then ...."
Walk with God to be holy, upright.

27.

Today you are the Lord's people,
You must do good, eschew evil.
When you're in the land,
'Rect stone-carved commands.
"Amen" each warning; don't wheedle.

28.

Commandments, statutes you'll obey
If you want life to go your way.
God's blessings are great,
His curses you'll hate.
Gratitude keeps God's wrath at bay.

---

* SILs are sisters-in-law, or in this case of Levirate marriage, widowed sisters in law.

** Note to self, men: Your wife may not grab your adversary's genitals when intervening in a fight.

29.

You've been graced with God's miracles.
Now, your fate's in these principles.
The deal with God's clear:
With joy you'll adhere,
Or be puked, like those previous fools.

30. *Nitzavim*/Standing (Witnessing)

It's not beyond you to succeed.
These words are near, so hear and heed.
The Lord's sake and yours,
Make these your days' chores,
So God keeps this promise, I plead.

31. *Vayelech*/And he went

At my age, one hundred and twenty,
I'm done. And Lord knows, I've seen plenty.
When Joshua and God
Lead your conquering squad,
You'll win. More? I'm no cognoscenti.*

31. *Ha'azinu*/Listen up

Ears up, skies! I'll drench earth with song.
God's perfect; it's we who've gone wrong.
Avenges, forgives –
Chosen people lives!
My Lord tells me to say, "So long."

---

* A person with special knowledge. While Israelites did not practice Italian while waiting to conquer Canaan, its Roman-Latin foundation probably makes this the closest my foreign language choices get to overlapping with this story.

32.   *V'zot Ha'brachah*/And this is the blessing

With a blessing for each leader,
God gave us love and this reader.
You twelve tribes stand here,
Gifts of each quite clear.
Glad Israel! Priests? Holy. Eager.

33.

He died in the end, great Moses,
No one knows where to send roses.
They mourned thirty days
His glorious ways.
And thus, our desert tale closes.

Hazak, Hazak va-Nit'hazek

Be strong, be strong and strengthen ourselves

> *We did it, read all the Five Books:*
> *Dense legalese, stories with hooks.*
> *Now be strong and rise*
> *For next year's reprise:*
> *Firmament, snake, heroes and schnooks.*

About the Author

Rhonda Rosenheck holds a BA in English Literature and Rhetoric from Binghamton University and an MEd in Jewish Education from the Jewish Theological Seminary of America. She studied at Hebrew College in Newton, MA, completed a graduate fellowship at the Hebrew University in Jerusalem, and studied Applied Linguistics in a Master's Program at Nova Southeastern University. Rhonda's publications include a poetry chapbook titled *Looking: Out, Up, In & Under Rocks* (Elephant Tree House Press 2018), a self-published chapbook entitled *Sin No More! A Biblical Sea Shanty* (2020) and an illustrated book of humor titled *Yiddische Yoga: OYsanas for Every Generation* (ill., Dana Toons, Ben Yehuda Press, 2016). Retired from religious educational leadership and again from a copyediting business, Rhonda writes and operates a writer's retreat near the Mohawk River. She lives just outside Albany, NY.

The Jewish Poetry Project

jpoetry.us

Ben Yehuda Press

From the Coffee House of Jewish Dreamers: Poems of Wonder and Wandering and the Weekly Torah Portion by Isidore Century

"Isidore Century is a wonderful poet. His poems are funny, deeply observed, without pretension." – *The Jewish Week*

The House at the Center of the World: Poetic Midrash on Sacred Space by Abe Mezrich

"Direct and accessible, Mezrich's midrashic poems often tease profound meaning out of his chosen Torah texts. These poems remind us that our Creator is forgiving, that the spiritual and physical can inform one another, and that the supernatural can be carried into the everyday."
—Yehoshua November, author of *God's Optimism*

we who desire: Poems and Torah riffs by Sue Swartz

"Sue Swartz does magnificent acrobatics with the Torah. She takes the English that's become staid and boring, and adds something that's new and strange and exciting. These are poems that leave a taste in your mouth, and you walk away from them thinking, what did I just read? Oh, yeah. It's the Bible."
—Matthue Roth, author, *Yom Kippur A Go-Go*

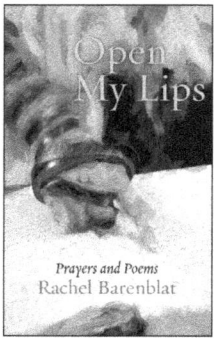

Open My Lips: Prayers and Poems by Rachel Barenblat

"Barenblat's God is a personal God—one who lets her cry on His shoulder, and who rocks her like a colicky baby. These poems bridge the gap between the ineffable and the human. This collection will bring comfort to those with a religion of their own, as well as those seeking a relationship with some kind of higher power."
—Satya Robyn, author, *The Most Beautiful Thing*

Words for Blessing the World: Poems in Hebrew and English by Herbert J. Levine

"These writings express a profoundly earth-based theology in a language that is clear and comprehensible. These are works to study and learn from."
—Rodger Kamenetz, author, *The Jew in the Lotus*

Shiva Moon: Poems by Maxine Silverman

"The poems, deeply felt, are spare, spoken in a quiet but compelling voice, as if we were listening in to her inner life. This book is a precious record of the transformation saying Kaddish can bring."
—Howard Schwartz, author, *The Library of Dreams*

is: heretical Jewish blessings and poems by Yaakov Moshe (Jay Michaelson)

"Finally, Torah that speaks to and through the lives we are actually living: expanding the tent of holiness to embrace what has been cast out, elevating what has been kept down, advancing what has been held back, reveling in questions, revealing contradictions."
—Eden Pearlstein, aka eprhyme

Texts to the Holy: Poems
by Rachel Barenblat

"These poems are remarkable, radiating a love of God that is full bodied, innocent, raw, pulsating, hot, drunk. I can hardly fathom their faith but am grateful for the vistas they open. I will sit with them, and invite you to do the same."
—Merle Feld, author of *A Spiritual Life*

The Sabbath Bee: Love Songs to Shabbat
by Wilhelmina Gottschalk

"Torah, say our sages, has seventy faces. As these prose poems reveal, so too does Shabbat. Here we meet Shabbat as familiar housemate, as the child whose presence transforms a family, as a spreading tree, as an annoying friend who insists on being celebrated, as a woman, as a man, as a bee, as the ocean."
—Rachel Barenblat, author, *The Velveteen Rabbi's Haggadah*

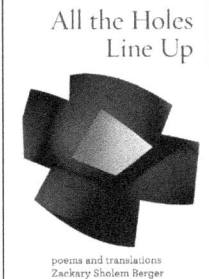

All the Holes Line Up: Poems and Translations
by Zackary Sholem Berger

"Spare and precise, Berger's poems gaze unflinchingly at—but also celebrate—human imperfection in its many forms. And what a delight that Berger also includes in this collection a handful of his resonant translations of some of the great Yiddish poets." —Yehoshua November, author of *God's Optimism* and *Two World Exist*

How to Bless the New Moon: The Priestess Paths Cycle and Other Poems for Queens
by Rachel Kann

"To read Rachel Kann's poems is to be confronted with the possibility that you, too, are prophet and beloved, touched by forces far beyond your mundane knowing. So, dear reader, enter into the 'perfumed forcefield' of these words—they are healing and transformative."
—Rabbi Jill Hammer, co-author of *The Hebrew Priestess*

Into My Garden
by David Caplan

"The beauty of Caplan's book is that it is not polemical. It does not set out to win an argument or ask you whether you've put your tefillin on today. These gentle poems invite the reader into one person's profound, ambiguous religious experience."
—*The Jewish Review of Books*

Between the Mountain and the Land is the Lesson: Poetic Midrash on Sacred Community
by Abe Mezrich

"Abe Mezrich cuts straight back to the roots of the Midrashic tradition, sermonizing as a poet, rather than ideologue. Best of all, Abe knows how to ask questions and avoid the obvious answers."
—Jake Marmer, author, *Jazz Talmud*

NOKADDISH: Poems in the Void
by Hanoch Guy Kaner

"A subversive, midrashic play with meanings—specifically Jewish meanings, and then the reversal and negation of these meanings."
—Robert G. Margolis

An Added Soul: Poems for a New Old Religion
by Herbert Levine

"These poems are remarkable, radiating a love of God that is full bodied, innocent, raw, pulsating, hot, drunk. I can hardly fathom their faith but am grateful for the vistas they open. I will sit with them, and invite you to do the same."
—Merle Feld, author of *A Spiritual Life*.

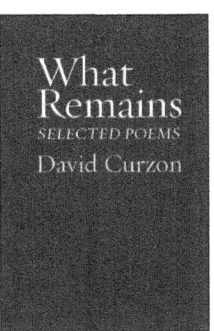

What Remains
by David Curzon

"Aphoristic, ekphrastic, and precise revelations animate WHAT REMAINS. In his stunning rewriting of Psalm 1 and other biblical passages, Curzon shows himself to be a fabricator, a collector, and an heir to the literature, arts, and wisdom traditions of the planet."
—Alicia Ostriker, author of *The Volcano and After*

The Shortest Skirt in Shul
by Sass Oron

"These poems exuberantly explore gender, Torah, the masks we wear, and the way our bodies (and the ways we wear them) at once threaten stable narratives, and offer the kind of liberation that saves our lives."
—Alicia Jo Rabins, author of *Divinity School*, composer of *Girls In Trouble*

Walking Triptychs
by Ilya Gutner

These are poems from when I walked about Shanghai and thought about the meaning of the Holocaust.

Book of Failed Salvation
by Julia Knobloch

"These beautiful poems express a tender longing for spiritual, physical, and emotional connection. They detail a life in movement—across distances, faith, love, and doubt."
—David Caplan, author, *Into My Garden*

Daily Blessings: Poems on Tractate Berakhot
by Hillel Broder

"Hillel Broder does not just write poetry about the Talmud; he also draws out the Talmud's poetry, finding lyricism amidst legality and re-setting the Talmud's rich images like precious gems in end-stopped lines of verse."
—Ilana Kurshan, author of *If All the Seas Were Ink*

The Missing Jew: Poems 1976-2022
by Rodger Kamenetz

"How does Rodger Kamenetz manage to have so singular a voice and at the same time precisely encapsulate the world view of an entire generation (also mine) of text-hungry American Jews born in the middle of the twentieth century?"
—Jacqueline Osherow, author, *Ultimatum from Paradise* and *My Lookalike at the Krishna Temple: Poems*

The Red Door: A dark fairy tale told in poems
by Shawn Harris

"THE RED DOOR, like its poet author Shawn C. Harris, transcends genres and identities. It is an exploration in crossing worlds. It brings together poetry and story telling, imagery and life events, spirit and body, the real and the fantastic, Jewish past and Jewish present, to spin one tale."
—Einat Wilf, author, *The War of Return*

The Matter of Families
by Robert Deluty

"Robert Deluty's career-spanning collection of New and Selected poems captures the essence of his work: the power of love, joy, and connection, all tied together with the poet's glorious sense of humor. This book is Deluty's masterpiece."
—Richard M. Berlin, M.D., author of *Freud on My Couch*

www.ingramcontent.com/pod-product-compliance
Lightning Source LLC
LaVergne TN
LVHW041343080426
835512LV00006B/595